"My Little Letter Case"

The Jamaican Edition

A compilation of letters on current
affairs written by the author between
2001 and 2009

CANUTE WHITE

MSc (Psy), MSc (Org. Stud.), BSc

Independently published
Miramar, Florida
My Little Letter Case: The Jamaican Edition
Copyright © 2019 Canute White
All rights reserved

First edition (Jamaican Edition)
Printed in the United States
ISBN: 9781098508302

Dedicated to my wife
Cadene Cole-White; MBA, BS
who was extremely supportive

LETTER 1

Truth, right and wrong
Tuesday, July 24, 2001

Dear Public;

There is usually a propensity for wanting to hear "two sides of the story", but a trend has developed, which forced me to coin the phrase, "opposing truth". Can there be two different truths to a story? If two people are telling the truth, yet opposing each other at the same time, then there is an indication of a lie (a liar) somewhere. The situation, in effect, becomes confusing until an investigation is conducted -- indeed, by clean and 'unbiased' hands. This concept of opposing truth is often used, maybe ostentatiously, in domestic and political conflicts.

The perception of rightness depends on accepted moral and operational principles; therefore, what is right to one person may not be right to another. However, rightness should be evaluated according to the outcome of the action(s). Care should be taken though; that what is right is not seen as wrong and the wrong seen as right. It is important that the modus operandi and responding attitudes toward conflicts be approached with rightness, taking into consideration the need for an appropriate outcome.

There can only be one truth to any story, even if it is being uttered by two sides vying for truth. The other 'truth' is a lie.

Reader's Response:

LETTER 2

Hatred: Is it a weapon?
Tuesday, December 18, 2001

Dear Public;

I have read a magazine article in which the writer described hatred as a weapon. The writer also stated that human nature has equipped mankind with this weapon. As implied by the article, the writer's opinion was prompted by the recent attack on America.

This interesting concept on hatred has forced me to consult my Oxford dictionary in order to find the meaning of "weapon". According to the dictionary, "weapon" is a thing designed or used for inflicting harm or damage. So, is hatred a weapon?

Hatred is an emotion, displayed or hidden, which causes psychological harm or damage to another. The psychological effect depends on the relationship between the one who hates and the victim of that hatred. If a child blatantly hates his mother, this would inflict psychological harm to the mother. Hatred is a psychological weapon.

The spate of murder in our society is evidently an effect of hatred being directly used to inflict damage on the social well-being and security of a people. Hatred is a weapon used against society. It is a weapon created by the supposed inability to deal with social conflicts and the unwillingness to accept or allow the ideologies -- political, social or religious -- of others.

Hatred is the weapon, which points the guns, issues injustice and neglects. It perpetrates all manner of crime 'against the person'. In effect, hatred inflicts harm and damage to humanity.

Reader's Response:

LETTER 3

Men are at risk
Tuesday, October 23, 2001

Dear Public;

Compton's New Century Encyclopaedia and Reference Collection II defines "risk" as the chance of injury, damage, or loss; dangerous chance; hazard. Men are extremely vulnerable, based on societal factors, which place them at risk.

The inability of some men to fulfil societal expectations forces them to become deviants. Men who are not able to provide for their families, because of unemployment, or some other factors, may resort to crime. This may place them in jail and rob them of their self-esteem. Societal acceptance, somehow, depends on one's ability to fulfil societal expectations.

Men are viewed, based on the spate of crime in the society, as more harmful than women. This view has placed men at risk as they are ignored, even when they genuinely need help. Women will certainly receive assistance without any expression of hesitation.

I would like to suggest that the "nakedness" displayed by some women also place men at risk. This ostentatious attitude creates a potential for lust and is also an invitation for crime of an abusive nature. Most men have a propensity to misinterpret the non-verbal, physical language of women and push themselves into incarceration.

One cannot excuse the rapid establishment of bars and drug bases in our society as a contributing factor to the

11

concept of "men at risk". This is an opportunity to create more alcohol and drug abusers among the male population of the society. The increase in these establishments increases vulnerability.

The factors that place men at risk are rapidly increasing and risk becomes inevitable. Another man will start drinking alcohol and using cocaine right now. Today another man will drift into promiscuity. Let's face it, men are at risk.

Reader's Response:

LETTER 4

Expulsion extreme
Monday, January 14, 2002

Dear Public;

One's attitude can only be changed through education and persuasion. The concept of persuasion becomes more effective when the ones being persuaded are also being educated about the advantages of accepting the persuasion. Based on this, I believe that the Munro boys, involved in the ganja-smoking saga, should be given a chance to be educated. This will, in effect, induce a chance to develop a changed attitude.

Despite attending St George's College, I must confess that I have always admired Munro for its high academic standard and level of

14

discipline; therefore, Munro's board members should view Munro as one of the ideal institutions for attitude change through education and persuasion. The boys should be viewed as "material" to work with, instead of "material" to be discarded for further deterioration.

Suspension would be appropriate but to expel the boys is an extreme approach to discipline, in this regard. It would be interesting to see the school's code of conduct and relative code of discipline. Expulsion would create problems for the boys to be admitted into other educational institutions, thus affecting the boys' quest to obtain high quality education. Schools, I suppose, take the recommendations of other schools seriously. What would have been the content of Munro's recommendations regarding the boys it had thrown out?

Come on Munro, educate for change. Take comfort in having those boys re-instated and you will be commended, and surprised, for what they will become in this society, because of the effort of a "caring" institution. The public is watching.

Reader's Response:

LETTER 5

Teach conflict management in schools

Tuesday, June 04, 2002

Dear Public;

The recent spate of violence in the schools is an indication of the high level of indiscipline in the society. It is also a reflection of most students' inability to deal with social conflicts. With this in mind, it would be reasonable to suggest that conflict management courses be taught in schools, starting at the primary level. In addition, a conflict management department should also be established in every educational institution.

Courses such as "Social problem solving" and "Conflict resolution" would contribute to the reduction of violence in the schools. The knowledge gleaned from those courses would generate a positive impact on the students. This impact would eventually change their attitude, hence the establishment of a peaceful school environment, which would be conducive to effective learning and development.

A student who is exposed to conflict management courses would understand the nature of conflicts and the appropriate methods to be employed in dealing with them. Those courses would equip the students with the skills necessary for negotiation and mediation in order to ensure peace. It would also allow the students to recognise that people do not have problems with people. Instead, people have problems with issues. However, people are necessary components of those issues.

A conflict management department would operate like the guidance-counselling department in that it deals with social issues. However, guidance counsellors are not conflict managers and therefore lack the expertise in conflict resolution. All schools should establish a department, adequately staffed and equipped, with the sole responsibility to intervene in violent confrontations in order to ensure a rational resolution.

Education administrators should view the concept of conflict management, in the schools, as one method in dealing with the spate of school violence. Establish a conflict management department, which is as important as guidance-counselling department, and educate, in conflict management, to change the attitude of students. This could ensure peace.

Reader's Response:

LETTER 6

Politics, wealth, education
Tuesday, September 24, 2002

Dear Public;

Jamaica is currently in an atmosphere which is conducive to political, theatrical episodes leading to the general election. Those episodes would, no doubt, include a plethora of criticisms regarding the credentials of prospective candidates. The critical issues which may emerge are the intellectual capabilities of the candidates, also their wealth. Nevertheless, would it be logical to ignore appropriate, innate or learnt leadership qualities in exchange for wealth and mere eloquence, which may be acquired through educational achievements?

The concept of wealth, in this regard, is based on the hope that the candidate would be able to assist in the development of the constituency, through personal financial contributions. The candidate's personal wealth would not be the only "financial reservoir". Fiscal allotments would also be available to candidates and should be adequate for the effective management of constituencies. Personal wealth is not an essential criterion for effective leadership or appropriate political candidacy.

The radical need for an educated candidate is merely a reflection of the need for eloquence in public which is expected by the electorate and would contribute to the sustenance of "party image". However, not all educated people are eloquent. While educational achievements are essential requirements for a career in politics, mere eloquence should not be paramount.

Behind the lack of wealth and eloquence could be an ability to lead, organize and motivate a constituency, through effective management.

Reader's Response:

LETTER 7

Let's build now
Thursday, October 24, 2002

Dear Public;

Now that the parody of political campaigns and the surprises of general elections are over, it is time to continue the process of nation building, which requires a non-partisan concerted effort. Such effort should elicit essential ideas from across party borders for Jamaica to move forward as a nation.

The manifestos of the political parties need to be perused and amended to produce an amalgamated manifesto geared towards the formation of a fluid society. This suggestion is based on the consideration that the two manifestos are fraught with relevant ideas. This process of perusal and amendment should be scrutinised by politically unbiased individuals.

The leadership of the political parties, including the "third parties", need to collaborate, in a "non-parliamentary" assembly, on national developmental issues. This would allow the injection of diverse ideas into nation building. Based on the notion that political leaders are the microcosm of the society, this act of collaboration would create a model of friendship and unity for the supporters of the political parties.

As the nation's political sector transforms, after a general election, the attitudes of political magnates also require transformation in order to ensure a collaborative approach to nation building.

Reader's Response:

LETTER 8

Eradicating workplace conflicts

Monday, October 28, 2002

Dear Public;

The workplace should not only be a place which is operationally conducive to productivity, but it should also be a place in which the workers feel a sense of contentment, hence, creating a push factor for productivity.

The onus is "vested" in management to eradicate conflicts between management and employees, as well as among employees. Conflicts in the workplace are critical issues, which are neglected by most employers, in both the private and public sectors.

To eradicate workplace conflicts, whilst exerting influence, managers should also exert a level of respect for their employees. For instance, the attitude of shouting, if such action is necessary, should be an "office affair" and not an embarrassing display power in front of the department's staff. Such embarrassment could affect the victim's self-esteem and level of productivity. Undeniably, this would affect the organisation's productivity and, eventually, the image of management.

The absence of a conflict management department creates a serious deficiency in the workplace. This department should be headed by a trained conflict manager who would report to the human resource manager. Employees should be persuaded to trust the conflict management department as a refuge for resolution during employees' conflicts, which would curtail production through misuse of time, shift to "rowdiness".

The eradication of workplace conflicts will increase productivity and create a sense of contentment for employees. Nevertheless, the achievement of this task rests in the hands of management, ultimately, for the sake of the organization.

Reader's Response:

LETTER 9

Summit should have included "third parties"
Monday, November 11, 2002

Dear Public;

The first political summit, which was held recently at the prime minister's official residence (Vale Royal), is undoubtedly a prelude for political, economic and social changes in the society. The cordiality and seeming co-operation displayed among the participants indicated a transformation in the nation's political sector.

Based on media reports, the main political parties have agreed on national developmental issues. Constitutional reform, which was one of the issues discussed, is an important element in any discussion geared towards national development, as a changing society would require changes in its constitution, in order to "shift" the provisions of the constitution in sync with a fluid society and changing societal worldview.

The establishment of sub-committees, with members who are drawn from both parties, to conduct "extra-summit" discussions, on specific issues, is a great idea, which will bear fruit. Nevertheless, there is a pitfall, which the summit organisers should have borne in mind. The summit should have included participants from the "third parties".

It is said that the responsibility of government is to ensure the social well-being of the population. The principle is indeed logical. However, the social well-being of the population is the responsibility of every politician - government and Opposition(s). The summit conference is a source for change.

Reader's Response:

LETTER 10

Christmas vs general elections

Tuesday, January 07, 2003

Dear Public;

It may seem absurd to even entertain the thought that Christmas can be compared to general elections, as defined in this society. This absurdity may be based on the belief that Christmas and election are to be placed on separate extremes on the "continuum" of life's events. Nevertheless, Christmas is analogous to general elections.

The spate of unusual spending in preparation for Christmas, each year, can be likened to the spate of unusual spending, which characterizes the campaign period leading to general elections every five years. It doesn't

38

matter who spend. The issue is based in the plethora of funds released days before Christmas day and Election Day. In addition, Santa Clause is a symbol of Christmas and, in a sense, a symbol of elections. Maybe the election Santa is less of a myth than the Christmas Santa; but their intentions are somewhat, similar -- generosity. However, their pursuits are undeniably different. Christmas Santa gives support and Election Santa garners support.

Television commercials are an inescapable feature of the Christmas season, likewise a feature of election campaigns. The dramatic episodes of Christmas commercials are no different from those released by political parties during the campaign periods. These commercials are geared towards selling party image, mercantile goods and services.

Like Christmas Day, Election Day comes and goes and more "energy" is put into preparation, for the day, than the energy exerted on the day per se. At the end of Christmas day, like election day, the society returns to its routine. Waiting for another Christmas Day and another election day.

Reader's Response:

LETTER 11

Chance for political unity
Thursday, June 26, 2003

Dear Public;

The ultimate result of the recently held local government election has carved a new political landscape for Jamaica. This political re-design has created shared responsibilities for the two major political parties, hence a chance for political unity.

The fiscal dependency of the Opposition councilors should be honored by central government to satisfy the interest of the people. This would also allow the dismissal of any charge in relation to fiscal "holdbacks" and allow the councilors to perform their duties. In effect, central government provides the "cash" and local government (majority in the Opposition party) performs the "duties". This is a true sense of political unity.

The ultimate result should have left the government unperturbed; since such a result creates a concept of "specialization", which is a recipe for increased production, or growth. Decision making, regarding local government, is somewhat shifted to the Opposition party, hence allowing the government to concentrate solely on central government policies. Could this mean enhanced governance with resultant community development and economic growth?

It is important that the post-election dust be settled and that the work begins with the two major political parties collaborating in order to ensure effective governance in the interest of the Jamaican people.

Reader's Response:

LETTER 12

Fiscal autonomy v specialization
Tuesday, July 22, 2003

Dear Public;

The concept of "specialization", regarding a split in responsibility between central government and local government, which was mentioned in the article, "Chance for political unity", published in the Observer on Thursday, June 26, was criticized by a policy analyst from the United States. The criticism was posted on the newspaper's website via "Talk back comments on chance for political unity".

As the author of "Chance for political unity", it is reasonable to clarify a supposed misunderstanding and express support for the policy analyst's suggestion for fiscal autonomy in local government. "Chance for Political Unity" has argued that the ultimate result from the recently held local government elections has created a concept of "specialization". It was also argued that the provision of funds by central government (PNP) for local government (majority from JLP) to do the job is a true sense of political unity. The policy analyst considered this "analysis on local government", as it was called, to be flawed.

The concept of specialization refers to the existing situation and does not present an opposition, in any form, to the proposal of fiscal autonomy for local governance. In effect, fiscal autonomy for local governance is an excellent idea. Nevertheless, it would have changed the situation; therefore, make annulled the concept of specialization, as argued in the article. With fiscal autonomy, local governance would be more effective and timelier in its performance. The bureaucracy involved in "fiscal transfer" would be non-existent.

Reader's Response:

LETTER 13

Post office blues
Tuesday, September 16, 2003

Dear Public;

It was recently reported that several post offices could face closure as a result of the mercilessness of two well-established utility companies. As implied from media reports, the workers from the affected post offices have consented to continue the provision of excellent services, under "hardship", to the public.

This decision by the postal workers may be classified as altruistic; but could such altruism be narrowed to egotism (egoistic altruism) or is it an expression intended to "put people first"?

Although commendable, the concept of putting people first, in the absence of electricity and with a somewhat extreme exposure to heat, is a very difficult task. Ironically, putting the customers first in such conditions would create a level of discomfort for the customers. They should be "detoured" to other post offices for comfort and, as usual, great services.

With the prevalence of mobile phones, the disconnection of the fixed telephone lines should not have caused much burden on the postal staff or the people it serves. The Internet, which requires the fixed lines, is not an essential, but a welcome service being offered by the postal sector.

It is hoped that the action by the affected postal workers constitute real altruism and not one geared to ensure job

security, which could be threatened by
several closed post offices.

Reader's Response:

LETTER 14

Epidemic?
Wednesday, August 27, 2003

Dear Public;

It seems clearly unnoticeable, to the Ministry of Health, that there may be an imminent outbreak of a respiratory epidemic in the vicinity of the Riverton City Dump, on Spanish Town Road in Kingston. This would be the result of the smoke that has spread itself like a specter across communities, which include Seaview Gardens, Duhaney Park, Washington Gardens, and Waterhouse.

In the night, when hard-working people deserve to sleep, they are forced to stay awake because of their inability to breathe properly, in addition to coughing. The smoke becomes a trap as it would be senseless to open a window for a breath of fresh air.

The Ministry of Health needs to intervene in order to prevent a spate of respiratory diseases in the area. Experts should examine ways to prevent the smoke nuisance, which seems to have become a regular part of life for the affected communities.

Nevertheless, the Ministry of Health needs to send a team of public health workers to those communities in order to provide health education regarding preventative health measures.

Reader's Response:

LETTER 15

Justice, jury, and authority
Wednesday, December 28, 2005

Dear Public;

Justice is analogous to psychological constructs such as fear and anxiety, in as far as measurement is concerned. Justice cannot be measured directly because it is abstract in nature. However, there are observable elements which can indicate the absence or presence of justice and, in effect, the quality of justice. If this begs the question, quality refers to 'perceived' fairness of justice-based decisions.

Justice is defined by the Oxford English Dictionary as fairness or the exercise of authority in the maintenance of right. For clarification, the same source defined 'right' as the state of being entitled to a privilege or immunity. It is reasonable to suggest that in the justice system the jury, with its legal power, has a 'collective' authority to decide whether an accused person is guilty or not guilty. The jury is the authority that is vested with the onus to maintain legal rights. If given the chance to exercise its authority, the jury's decision must be respected and free from political and extended social dabbling.

It is no doubt, and rightly so, that people will be philosophical in their thinking patterns. Philosophical thinking is often based on interests and 'hypothesis', hence the existence of diverse perspectives on any issue, social or political. Is justice, in regard to judicial proceedings, the responsibility of the government or the jury, which is a microcosm of the ordinary citizens in the society?

The appropriate and acceptable quality of any single jury mechanism, by virtue of adequate screening, pursued with a high level of validity, is one reason to accept its final decision.

Reader's Response:

LETTER 16

Start of a gender-based revolution at St George's

Tuesday, June 27, 2006

Dear Public;

The appointment of a female as principal of St. George's College has spurred discomfort among some of its stakeholders, and by extension, triggers the voice of at least one gender lobby group. As the debate continues, gender-based concerns, for some persons, become obvious. Now, it's clear that the fear surrounds the fact that a woman will be the head of a relatively all-male school.

It is no doubt that there is a level of shortsightedness regarding the ability of Jamaican women to perform on par with, or above, the capabilities of most men in the society. In effect, women must be given the chance to achieve based on meritocracy and not be pushed aside based on gender, and perhaps, personal issues, or regarding the notion that' "Only man can rule boys."

When one speaks of the strength of a man, it's perceived from the perspective of physical ability, but the strength of a woman is often perceived from the perspective of emotional stability and, to some extent, assertiveness and self-focused attitude. With this in mind, which is the best 'strength' for the psychology of boys? Women, too, can rule boys.

In addition to the increasing academic competence of women, especially in the disciplines of business administration and management, the strength and efficiency exerted in familial management, in most instances, without the male support or visibility, must be considered as a catalyst for rethinking the objection to a female principal for the North Street boys.

The 'matrifocalisation' of St. George's College is not a recipe for its demise, but the start of a 'gender-based' revolution, which cannot be prevented. As women become more educated and display a higher level of intellectual prowess than most men, more boy schools could have female heads of departments and principals, doing excellent jobs.

Reader's Response:

LETTER 17

The psychology of elections
Sunday, November 4, 2007

Dear Public;

The general election, and the anxiety which has characterized its aftermath, have gradually passed and soon, the society should be pushed into normality.

However, the process of ballot counting should be reviewed as the relevant authorities reflect on the discrepancies and pitfalls of the event. The process of ballot counting is undeniably a mental process, which requires concentration and psychological wellness.

It is no doubt reasonable to suggest that the fatigue created by a day of mental and physical rigidity would render the individual's incapable of performing with the required efficiency in counting the ballots, especially the same night after the electorate had voted.

The fatigue would have affected concentration and perhaps induced unintended seconds of napping, which would have been detrimental to the outcome of the counting process. In addition, the immediate anxiety caused by partisan 'social identity' and the 'waiting' for the outcome can affect the counting process as election workers are also part of the electorate, and no doubt, have normal vested interests in the results of the general election.

Reduce tensions

The individuals and the time of counting the ballots should be critically considered to reduce the tensions between partisan supporters and among the candidates of the major political parties.

First, it is a good idea to delay the counting of ballots until the day after the election. This would give the stakeholders some time to relax and perhaps reduce mental and physical tensions - ensuring efficiency in performing the process. Second, individuals involved in the counting should be specially selected and vetted to ensure unbiased attitudes - perhaps a cadre of clergymen and women.

The psychology of elections characterizes one aspect of political psychology that should be considered by the authorities and in such consideration, the psychological implications of ballot counting, especially as it relates to the counters, should be critically evaluated.

Reader's Response:

LETTER 18

Justice system must become crime fighter
Wednesday, August 6, 2008

Dear Public;

It seems paradoxical that a system, which is expected to correct a negative situation, may be a contributing factor to the sustenance of that situation. The justice system of Jamaica, which, in reality, constitutes the police with their investigative and enforcement responsibilities, the courts and the prisons, could be considered as a contributing factor to the spate of crime in the society. As absurd as it may seems, the inherent leniency exerted through the operations of the justice system unintentionally breeds the perpetration of crime.

Perhaps, the ingredients of the recently announced crime plan represented a recipe, which was aimed at addressing the relative flaws in the apparatus of the justice system. The plan adequately considered the issues of detention, bail and imprisonment, in its quest to ensure a level of deterrent, although not enough, from engagement in hard-core criminal activities.

The awareness of leniency that cannot be easily manipulated or eliminated by 'well-thinking' individuals, who serve in the police force, courts and correctional department of the justice system, creates recidivists and perhaps motivates criminal-minded individuals to make their debut into crime. In the minds of the perpetrators, and potential perpetrators, there is an almost sure possibility, based on personal and observable experiences, that the justice system and its relative laws would provide means of escape or just offer what may be considered 'bearable' sentences.

For the Jamaican justice system to be classified as a 'crime fighter', it needs to harden its heart, through the operations of the security forces, courts system, correctional services and in, indeed, the provisions in its laws. Some of these laws are useless for their own purposes and, therefore, need to be urgently amended to fight crime.

Dressings for the wounds

With that in mind, the terms of the crime plan seem relevant in order to provide dressings for the wounds of the justice system as it provides timely guidelines, which give more power to the system, in its quest to address the spate of crime in the society. It will no doubt be criticized because of the element of inequity in society and the resultant pulls between sides. In addition, no change will be readily accepted, especially by those whom it affects most. The crime plan will fill the gaps in the justice system and give it more teeth to deal with criminals and crime. Although it's not a panacea, let's see what the crime plan will do to ensure that the Jamaican justice system becomes a crime fighter instead of a crime contributor.

Reader's Response:

LETTER 19

A tricky notion
Wednesday, June 24, 2009

Dear Public;

The recent announcement by the minister of education on the Grade Four Literacy Test begs the question: Is the government contemplating a re-introduction of the Common Entrance Examination (CEE)? According to the minister, if a child failed to pass the literacy test after three sittings, that child would not be allowed to sit the Grade Six Achievement Test (GSAT). In my mind, there must be an institution, where the GSAT awardees do not attend, that would accept these failing students. Technically, as it is now, all secondary-level schools are for GSAT awardees.

Lack validity

The GSAT has been criticised as lacking validity and perhaps too difficult for the examinees grade and age levels. The science seems to be fraught with chemistry, biology and physics. The communication task is almost akin to CXC English language and the social studies to CXC social studies. It also seems unfair as each student gets only one chance to sit the test. Perhaps, it's also more difficult to get an acceptable average in the GSAT than it was to pass the CEE. The CEE was easier in content as the students would only be required to do some mental ability, mathematics and English language with a composition.

Needs re-examination

Whatever the situation, the GSAT must be re-examined in terms of its content validity and difficulty level.

The CEE should be reintroduced and those who pass go to the traditional high schools. The notion that every student passed is absurd and somewhat tricky. Something must be done as the system seems to be failing its students and not the students necessarily failing themselves.

Reader's Response:

LETTER 20

Don't use a broad-brush
Saturday, June 27, 2009

Dear Public;

The actions of clergymen exploiting their sexuality in socially unacceptable behaviour, as well as other 'illegal' sexual activities, must not be condoned. However, it would be a fallacy to suggest that the behaviour of one individual might be generalised to that individual's profession. It is wise to view people's actions as indicative of their own attitude and as such, apply 'individual meritocracy'.

Therefore, clergymen must be spared the stereotypical labelling and be seen as good and decent persons who are willing to maintain the integrity of their profession. In effect, pastors who solicit sex and/or sleep with minors should be seen as individuals with their own mindset and not necessarily microcosms of clergymen.

The media should place emphasis on the individual and not the individual's profession.

Reader's Response:

LETTER 21

Modernize the toll plazas
Tuesday, September 8, 2009

Dear Public;

It has been many years now since Jamaica established and developed toll plazas, perhaps to generate additional revenues, but more so to facilitate the haste and convenience of motorists. The operators must be commended for the services, which are being provided at these plazas, but more could be done to modernize these 'malls'.

First, an area of the Vineyard Toll Plaza could be allotted and franchised to a petrol station company in order to enhance the convenience. It is no secret that motorists whose vehicles 'suddenly' need a small amount of gasoline to get off the highway and into some nearby petrol station have been accommodated. Not bad, but the facility to full up may be more convenient. In addition, getting a snack under the same roof, as most petrol stations provide, would be appreciated.

Cash dispensers

Second, the same building could house an automatic teller machine (ATM) to dispense cash to motorists who have multilinked cards. It is not permitted to make U-turns around at the toll plazas and, therefore, not being able to locate all the cash that was saved for the toll could cause a long delay or do what is 'beyond the pale' for some persons - beg another motorist for a 'make up'. It would be more convenient to use the ATM if a card with adequate cash is accessible. However, the alternative is to upgrade the collection method. Why not have special lanes for payments by cards - credit or debit? Let's assume that most motorists are cardholders. The recent increase in toll would have caught many persons short of cash, forced to reverse from the cashier's window - trapped without cash.

Disturbing for motorists

Because of the fast-moving nature of toll plazas, the petrol station with its ATM modality could be placed strategically to avoid traffic congestion and loitering in the vicinity of the toll cashiers. Certainly, a long stretch of road without convenient gasoline dispensers and facility to get cash, especially for toll, is disturbing for motorists who are running out of gasoline and/or cash.

Reader's Response:

Thanks for reading my letters

I'm Yours

Truly;

Canute White

Jamaican National Anthem

Eternal Father bless our land
Guard us with Thy mighty hand
Keep us free from evil powers
Be our light through countless hours
To our leaders, Great Defender,
Grant true wisdom from above
Justice, truth be ours forever
Jamaica, land we love
Jamaica, Jamaica, Jamaica, land we love.

Teach us true respect for
Stir response to duty's call
Strengthen us the weak to cherish
Give us vision lest we perish
Knowledge send us, Heavenly Father,
Grant true wisdom from above
Justice, truth be ours forever
Jamaica, land we love
Jamaica, Jamaica, Jamaica, land we love

Jamaica National Pledge

Before God and all mankind, I pledge the
love and loyalty of my heart, the wisdom
and courage of my mind, the strength and
vigour of my body in the service of my
fellow citizens; I promise to stand up for
Justice, Brotherhood and Peace, to work
diligently and creatively, to think generously
and honestly, so that Jamaica may, under
God, increase in beauty, fellowship and
prosperity, and play her part in advancing
the welfare of the whole human race.